After All

Pat Daneman

FUTURECYCLE PRESS
www.futurecycle.org

Cover artwork, a photo by Pat Daneman; author photo by herself; cover and interior book design by Diane Kistner; Plantagenet Cherokee text and titling

Library of Congress Control Number: 2018952394

Published by FutureCycle Press
Athens, Georgia, USA

ISBN 978-1-942371-59-5

For Barry, Kathy, and David

Contents

4

1

I can't go back to yesterday—because I was a different person then.

—Lewis Carroll

The Women in the Kitchen

Go see the women in the kitchen,
who whisper to each other
while they cook. They'll let you in

and lift you up, squeeze you closer
as you pull their hairpins out
and curl your fingers through the silver

circles in their ears.
They know how to turn coal
smoke white as bed sheets, how

to sprinkle pain away with salt.
They will make a wall
of flesh around you, tell you

truths that make you wish
for tales—how little girls disappear
into kitchens, why

the big pot is kept
boiling, what the thing
inside it used to be.

Mother Song

When you have the mother who plays
the same Chopin étude on the piano
over and over until it is perfect
as a champagne bubble ascending
a crystal goblet, that is different

than when you have the mother who thinks
she is Callas and sings in her bedroom all day,
never goes outside, throws jars and bottles
at the door when the bell rings. Different

than the mother who lives in the house in between
these two, who is fat, whose hair is corkscrews,
whose hands are raw with wind and soap
as she pins white sheets on the line,
smiles at the clouds and tells you

they are in the shapes of rabbits today.
Later, she will take down the sheets, frozen
stiff as cardboard, smooth them warm and soft
against her belly, call you to help her fold in half,

in half again, a dance, until there is a pile
in the basket that she lifts onto her hip,
carries into the house as if it holds a baby
she found hidden under a bush.

First Communion Day

Morning is noisy with birds and restless
    with leaf shadows. My veil is loose;

the lace cuffs of my socks sag into my shoes.
    Pear blossoms float in the tulips like the torn pieces

of bread we throw in the lake for the ducks. My father lights a cigar,
    rolls down the car window. Grandma sneezes,

pulls a handkerchief out of her sleeve. I have confessed,
    but I am not cleansed. On Easter, I saw

Aunt Helen take money from my mother's purse.
    I have memorized the women's faces

in the pictures in my father's bottom drawer.
    My brother killed three ducklings, buried them

under the hedge. He will drown me if I tell, put spiders
    in my bed. I will get presents today—

I want a dog, but I will get *Lives of the Saints* and a figurine
    of St. Theresa holding flowers. She will live

in the dollhouse with Barbie and Midge, keep spiders
    out of my dreams. My hair was still wet

when my mother pulled the rollers out. My neck is sore.
    In church everyone rises, sits, kneels.

The priest punches himself three times in the chest
    like my brother punches me. We say the prayer

for the dead and the prayer for eternal happiness.
    The line to the altar is slow.

My stomach growls. Prayers swell in my mouth
    like lake-water bread.

The Salt Marsh

Sky the color of meat, moon the light
of hunger. No one had seen the three girls
for three days. Where were they? Jennifer
with her song of escape from everything—

plates empty and washing undone.
Maria wearing new shoes, and Alice
who'd caused it all, crying everywhere
Father Nicholas had touched her,

telling her jewel-crusted secret
until her friends were jealous.
They had candy from Woolworths,
three bags so full the wax paper

threatened to break. One had stolen
a lipstick, another a handful of blue
embroidery floss. The first place
their mothers looked was the garden

in back of the rectory. Father Nicholas,
handsome, picked flowers and promised
to intercede. Girls in green mud
up to their ankles, batwing chatter

of ocean one flat mile away,
sway and soft touch of cattails, gulls' eyes
swiveling. Jennifer knew about lampshades
stretched from the skin of dead babies.

Maria knew that Santa was real.
Alice had helped Father Nicholas
pull a rabbit out of his pants. Delicate
weight of mosquitoes, shoes waterlogged,

too heavy to wear. They were in no danger
in the salt marsh. No priests

with manicured nails, no old men
opening doors of old Fords to show them

the baby birds in their laps. No thorns,
no nails, nothing sharp but the saw grass
that sliced at their legs with thistle tongues.
It was a terrible adventure, the best

any of them would ever have.
Even as salt cracked like a fist against stone—
winters of ice and no ice, summers of mothers
dying, Father Nicholas dying, nobody's father,

unpriested. They never forgot that last night—
how they walked out filthy as boys,
singing the Mass: *Kyrie Eleison. Christe Eleison.*
They never forgot each other's names.

Coming of Age

I never came downstairs to anything
    but order. A house with no air

conditioning, but I knew there was worse:

the skinny girl with limp hair who befriended me in the cafeteria
    to whisper that her father wore her clothes. The singing

sisters with no father, mother fierce as a gunshot blasting them
    onto stage after stage with threats of no dinner and rats

    in a locked basement closet. The long belt
of my mother's robe hung short from the knot at her waist,

her hems frayed. Once a week everything washed and hung up to dry.
    Wash day, then bath day, then polish-your-shoes day.

Sometimes my mother hummed to herself as if no one was there.

My father lived at his workbench, sorted nails into baby food jars,
    made noises with hammers and saws.
        He would let me come in, but he made me
           sit on the floor in the corner. No talking.

I huffed mildewed basement air, hungry for the smell of sawdust.
To this day I haunt lumberyards, seeking the glances
    of bow-legged men with beards shaped like horseshoes—
        hungry for their rude stares

and their turning away.

There was the boy who sat next to me in homeroom,
    sheltering his loose-leaf notebook, leaning hard on his pencil
        to draw penises and hourglass shapes with breasts

above scribbled triangles from which fell bullets and drops of blood.
The girl who sat in the back, quietly masturbating.

There were the girls with no lunch money, the boys with no coats,
the teachers who ate peanut butter sandwiches out of brown bags
        and smoked pot in cars they'd been driving since high school—
            his sideburns, her mini-skirt.

I had no future, only today. I had no path, away or beyond,
only home—sun-stained bedding and all the ground beef I could eat,
        free toilet paper, free toothpaste. My brother

made fun of my armpit hair. I made fun of his
pitted face. My mother never once slapped me,

though I could feel, as if her grief were inside me,
        how much she wanted to,

how far she could see every time she looked into my eyes.

Boys Who Cut the Legs Off Box Turtles

You're sure these are the same two who smash
jack-o-lanterns up and down the street and name
your brother Four-Eyes and pinch your nipples
on the school bus, who steal baseball cards
kids have clothes-pinned to their bicycle spokes
and call them fairies when they cry. They come
at night over the fence into your backyard

to the pen with foil pie tins spilling lettuce,
the cement pool you helped your father pour
and shape where you like to wash the turtles' shells
because the water makes the orange markings
shine like the lid of your grandmother's jewelry box.
One leg off each of the babies. Both
hind legs off big Bo, which is the name

you'd give a dog if you had one. That morning
you go out to see how they are doing
with the lettuce and find them—beaks opening,
closing in panic that you do not understand
until you pick Bo up and see only his front legs
treading air. Your father promises if you take them
back to the woods where you caught them, new legs

will grow, so you do. You leave them under the bushes
near the pond, watch for a while as they do not move.
The next time you see those boys—who after
high school will be sent to Vietnam—you shoot them
your most unflinching evil eye, wish them missing
limbs and nightmares to help them think about
what they have done.

Polly's Mother Sang Opera

We heard her, never saw her—
voice like liquid in a glass, ice
crackling, cold condensing
on its curves as it slipped
through our fingers. We imagined
what we did not see—
black curls, lace dress, her face
a sad older version of Polly's.

Though what did older mean to us?
When you are sixteen there is no other age,
no other way to look than tempting,
from the pink on your lips to the space
that opens when you spread your legs,
tan all the way into your underpants.

As for the real woman, who could say
if she was ugly or more beautiful
than her daughter, or if there was a bottle
on the bedside table? No one was allowed
in Polly's house, even best friends
got no further than the front porch—
Polly leaning out, lifting her heavy hair.

From above, the flood
of music, dark forest
of words we did not understand.
At home our own mothers
ironing, sleeping, smoking,
while we stood at Polly's door,
not knowing what we were
waiting for.

Drop a Knife, Somebody's Coming

Lonely, my mother scattered knives
like salt, conjuring visitors
to ring the bell—the Czech dairyman
who sang like Sinatra and left blocks of wet cheese

and egg honeycombs on the top step.
The teenage paperboy, the dry cleaner's fat driver,
the brush man, smoothing his dark hair
as she unlocked the door. Handsome as a doctor

on the soaps, his eyes blacker
than my father's, his hand quicker
to cozy hers. He took his time opening his case,
lifting out brushes with a smile that had to ache,

his little mustache stretched from cheek to cheek.
She would ask questions to keep him
on the couch, her eye falling on this
or that. But the afternoon always ended

with no sale. She would remember
a salad to be started, an early train to be met,
a kitchen closet tangled with new brooms,
still full of swish and promise.

To My Father

I am here
because she
was there,
a little chilly
without her sweater,
her sweater
a little frayed at the cuffs,
drooping a little
on the back of a chair.
Your mother's kitchen—
smelling like soup,
vegetables
melting together,
round thighs of the table,
thud of white plates on cloth.
I am here
because she was there,
her auburn hair curled,
her lips pink,
because she believed
women were twigs and twine
in the dark surging
history of men.
I am here where
it is spring again,
spring in the branches,
nests woven frail and serene.
Where the she-robin ruffles
the red of her breast,
and from the west
descends a black storm.

The Holy

1. Friday

My mother meets Jesus in the produce aisle
at Food Lion. Side-burned door-to-door type,
he doesn't know a thing about avocados.
He thinks salsa is music, and he's right about that,
but she has to teach him that tomatoes must be
unbearably heavy to hold, onions the ones
with the dirtiest smiles. He invites her
to a party back at his place. She says no.
She's got a clogged drain, missing daughter,
a little fire and water damage to take care of.

2. Saturday

My mother is near the main stage
for the last show of a weekend reggae festival
when she runs into Jesus again. Not good
since she's looking for me, escaped from her
bonfire—teddy bear, rolling papers,
all the music—not just Jimi and Bob, but Mary,
Peter and Paul, ripped out of covers, bent,
broken, stirred into the heap of clothes shredded
on the floor. Gasoline flare. Days spent
erasing me and now she wants me back. Jesus
squeezes close to snag a bite off her chicken stick,
drips jerk juice onto her shoes. She wants
to ask him where I might be, but he won't stop
talking. *I am jumping up and down
on the trampoline of the universe. Night
is endless when you have no one
to cut up your fruit.* He blows
a kiss and disappears into the forest
of ganja and music and shambling feet.

3. Sunday

Crimson, burgundy, flame, my mother's
bad dreams as she tosses in the slough
of her sheets beside the still body
of Jesus. Burnt umber the skin
of Seamus Greenheron, who stars
as the Savior in the new documentary-in-progress:
My Life in the Light. One of my hands
down his pants, the other smoothing the feathers
of the velvet-rooster back of his neck.
He smells like torn cotton. His mouth
tastes like the street. His body's a boat
with enough room to hold my whole tribe
of reasons for running away. I've given him
all of my money. I don't need any money.
I need my tongue and my hips. I need
a cellar to shut him in, a ladder to climb him. He's just
what I want what I want what I want.

Maybe This World

Is broken,
the stepping stones
in the creek
set too far apart.
Your foot
gets wet in between,
and your bare sole
catches an old hook
floating
its filament wisp.

Maybe your grandma
is baking *kuchen*
today, lifting it
in quilted hands
from the black mouth
of the white stove.
Maybe your father
is taking your mother's hand
or turning on the TV
while the man
with sticks in his beard
slides one finger
inside your blouse.

Maybe this world
is a book,
pages torn out
one by one,
laid down side by side,
waiting to be blown away
the next time
the crazy sky
opens.

2

The trouble was not in the kitchen or the tulips but only in my head...

—Anne Sexton

Kiss

I want that kiss—the one that starts
at my mouth but doesn't stop
until it's untied my shoes

and unbuckled my belt. That kiss
that tastes of purple jam
and sweet wind blown in

from California. I want that kiss
that spreads me like wings, that stops
a song on my lips. That kiss I know

is happening at this moment—
at the top of a subway stair,
on a secondhand couch in a garage apartment,

confident, wet with breath. A triumphant,
difficult kiss. I want that kiss—
wolves drawn to the edge

of the light, waves crashing
in darkness. I want that kiss—
I want to paint my lips pink

and print them all over
the shocked white face of the moon.

Adam and Eve

Standing naked in the guest room,
my new husband accuses me

of calling God a man and a know-it-all.
A man like any other man, I say.

It is late. Long past one of the last
midnights of October.

Furtive as mice, we have been down
to my mother's kitchen, crammed our mouths

with leftover meat and cake,
washed plates and set them back on shelves

to leave no evidence of hunger.
Upstairs, we try questions on like costumes

until we are naked, almost a pair.
Why, he asks me,

did God not question the serpent?
Because God thought he knew everything, I answer.

Lady of the House

Husband gone
to work, it's time

to let the madmen
out, ask them to help

slice cabbages. Children
at school, I bend back

covers of books,
peer inside empty

heads of dolls. Fat dove
at the window, color

of dishwater—so many
ways to bring the outside

in—fistful of flour,
silent, slow.

Last night as the moon
rose, the cat went

out. I envy
his muddy boots,

old blood
matting his chin—

me with my
kitchen canisters.

Soup

Tomorrow I will make soup.
Giant cabbages. A cut of pork
long as a fence post. Carrots and potatoes
that will hang like stars in my deep
bouillon dark. Soup big enough for two
pots. The storm we've been expecting
will pull into the driveway.
Long coat and bare feet, groaning
from the trip. Footprints
to fall asleep in. By afternoon we will give up
trying to keep the sidewalk clear. We will slide
out of focus, turn into the soft glow
under a shade. Fireflies in a jar.
In our tightly lidded house,
soup steaming, onions taking off
their clothes to roll in oily surf,
we will turn into summer.

Stage Four, Summer

Because my mother liked the colors of vegetables,
she cooked. And every day she rode her bike
around the ball field—though, by August,

only around the block—and she knew,
as she snapped the padlock shut,
that the last day was the last day.

She baked zucchini bread and read magazines
and cooked eggplant and tomatoes, green beans
and summer squash. She walked out for the mail,

drank tea, and learned things her doctors didn't know—
how the bedroom carpet felt against her cheek,
how with the telephone not ringing, music

could climb hills inside her head, color them
bright green as with a child's hand.
Backwards and forwards she learned the alphabet

of her dreams and how to dream
with eyes open. Day and night she watched
the sky. She thought about autumn coming—her bones

rattling against her clothes, bald pumpkins
scattered like teeth in the fields,
as gardens everywhere died.

Homecoming

Some places never change no matter how long you stay away—
this village of green-shuttered houses, for example. Colonial cemeteries,
autumn-dark streets. Across from the funeral parlor, the coffee shop

with the same swarthy waitresses who served you thirty years ago,
voile aprons and crepe soles unsticking from spilled syrup.
You can look through the window of Klein's and see yourself

in the mirror where you tried on prom dresses. The seamstress
at the tailor's wears a pincushion on her wrist like a corsage.
At the toy store, the wooden floor creaks, and no one will ever buy

the dusty marionette. The red and white sign swings over the grocery
in your old neighborhood: *Since 1927.* The man at the register
is gray and small, but he has a voice you recognize. He reaches

across the counter to take your hand, and you let him,
because he calls you by your mother's name—a mistake
you hide, like the penny candies you used to steal.

What Is Love?

In December the buildings here take on the colors
of stones on a western beach. Unprotected
by leafy shade the sidewalks turn the colors
of winter coats, animal hides. Shutters

across all the doors, awnings
that throw shadows the color of wet brick.
On the grass an untrampled sprinkle
of snow, crust of ice unbroken. Trees

painted in with a brush dipped in black.
The plume of a fountain the only thing
moving for blocks in any direction. Green
water shivers in its heated circle. For hours

only the bakers have been awake.
No traffic, no joggers winter-wrapped,
no walkers, no shoppers, no summer
kisses, only the muffled noise, now

and then, of a truck on the highway
like the sound of the neighbors upstairs.
Soon some of us will stutter from our beds,
comb out the night's promises.

Stomachs uncertain, cheeks creased,
we'll splash water on our faces, think coffee
is love. And snow, if the sun will shine
on it. And bread, in its blanket of heat.

I Speak at My Mother's Funeral

Without a net I rise up through a lake of eyes.

Words crumbling on wet paper. I
need the ink to move like clouds do

on a windy day into some order even
as they are about to fall over the horizon.

Frozen glances hang from me like hooks. I turn,
they turn. I've tried to calm myself with roses, books

and too much wine. My mother, Sunday-dressed
and rouged. I have never felt so less

alone. Before I start to speak I know
that I will fail to raise the dead—I move

my eyes past each of them—father, brothers, friends—one
yawns, another checks his watch. Later they will stop me

in the aisle—hands on my flesh, lips on my face,
thinking I don't feel the barbs as they release

me, drop back inside their serge.

Dreams of Dead Women

Dead women dream of daylight,
day moon white as a pillow.
Dream of walking unclothed,

cigarettes between glossy lips,
smoke asking its questions.
They want dishes to wash,

water too hot, weightless flight
of soap bubbles. They dream
of unhappy daughters, heavy quilts

folded back, the satisfaction of seeds
teased from their teeth. They want
pockets to mend, splinters to pull,

triumph of breath on their necks.
They want to hear their own footsteps on stairs,
feel dust shudder in corners.

In the Middle of the Night

No one is there for anyone else. Even though that is what we expected.
All over the city millions of people guarding their worries
like angels. People who don't deserve worries. People living in boxes.
People inexperienced with the politics of worry—should they go to the window
or into the kitchen? Is it time for a glass of wine?

The disappointing parent would make a list here.
Airplanes arriving or not arriving on time or not arriving at all.
Lumps that might be discovered, lightning bolts that might strike.

At this ridiculous hour the disappointing parent is asleep,
alone, or with someone disturbing. It is the waitress,
the public relations doyenne, the ammunition salesman we need
to consult at this moment. Haggard in the light of computer screens,
blue faces, fingers searching for answers to sleep-
withering questions.

Slim and cool, the bare feet of the understudy across the creaking wood floor
of her jealous mother-in-law's library. Locked in a bathroom
the assistant professor contemplates the shell-pink complexion
of his most promising student. They conspire,

water spills. Everywhere, longing. The young talk show producer
whose illness is taking its time. Her lover's prayers into the sky—
I'm afraid. You must try. Don't let go. Glasses on nightstands,
magazines slithered away.

Too late to the party last night, nobody ate your cheap cheese. No one cared
that you won the Missouri Award or that your doctor found nothing
worth keeping an eye on. All over the city good hosts, ugly dancers,
bankers with sore necks are writing notes to themselves.
Petting cats. Whistling. Millions of people are lying
awake, tugging at quilts heavy with the must

of ancestral insomnia. As clocks chime, as bells toll,
they send flaming or laundered or half-eaten wishes
like paper boats into darkness. As trucks hurl their weight
down innocent highways. As the earth moves and the sky
is still. As morning approaches.

Come Inside

There's no more work to be done in this weather. Come inside.
Turn the radio on; let it play all winter. Reacquaint yourself
with the feel of your head uncovered. Take your wool sweater

from the doorknob—button in. What is that song
that always makes you smile? Words that taste like ice
cream on your tongue. What is that melody that always
makes you turn the radio up loud? Music with hills in it,
sunflowers, gates. How you and she used to dance.
You in your socks, slipping on the linoleum,

she with eyes closed, fingertips matched to yours.
Who was she? Now and then you thought you knew.
Now and then you'd be sharing a pot of tea, laughing
at a newspaper story, and she would do something
with her hand or a tilt of her head and become unfamiliar,

exciting. Why do beds insist on being made? Yesterday
you bent to lift a blanket from the floor. Something caught
your eye. Cocooned in feathery dust, almost unreachable, one
of her earrings, gold, in the shape of a star. You can picture her
wearing it, can't remember if she'd ever said it was lost.

Phone Call from a Movie Set Somewhere in Kansas

My son is learning at last everything I never taught him.
He's learning to do whatever he's told by anyone
whose job it is to order up the impossible:
Tomorrow, David, it must not rain.
This Indian, David, he is six inches too tall.

He woke up one night standing outside a Best Western motel,
an old woman slapping him with a pillowcase, with motherly consternation,
scolding him in Spanish. He says he needs to learn Spanish.
And carpentry. So many things have to be built.
Difficult things that do not exist. A device for spitting
tobacco into someone's face, for example.
A house that falls down.

He sent me a postcard, he says. Sent his sister a postcard.
His grandfather a postcard. To his own mailbox hanging empty
at the door of his empty apartment he sent a postcard of a rampaging mare
he found wedged in the mirror in the toilet of a Texaco station
near Cottonwood Falls. It is his calling to find things; his station
in the underground maze where all the circuitry hums. He tells me
a Kiowa girl wrote a poem on his arm with a coyote tooth. A ghost

wrote a song in the dust on the hood of his car. His car wouldn't start
and Queen Bey stepped down from a red pickup truck, from her parapet
of sixty years and skin like hammered copper and blues
and jazz in all the cities of Europe to touch his face
with a varnished fingernail, give him a Diet Coke and a ride.

On an undulating plain at purple dawn he found a cowry shell
grimed with ocean salt. A herd of bison rose like a swarm of locusts
to consume a hilltop; beat a cloud from their hooves
that changed the color of the sky.

Nothing is lost, but so many things have to be found.

3

This is the Hour of Lead—
Remembered, if outlived,
As Freezing persons recollect the Snow—
First—Chill—then Stupor—then the letting go—

—Emily Dickinson

How It Rained in Barcelona

Mornings so hot we made no plans, spent hours
reading in the square. We sipped water, had no thoughts

of making lunch or love until that first gust brought a graying
to the sky, turned each leaf a deeper green. A moment

of expectation before a curtain dropped. Rain bright
on shingles, loud down drain pipes, soft, then gone,

as children came from everywhere to splash
along the cobblestones, flap pigeon hands and shriek—

that same joy we wanted to be feeling—as wind swung
every branch until it seemed like rain was falling still.

Since Diagnosis

The cups have stepped out of the cabinets—
they stand around on counters
like uncles, much to say and nothing new,

the slurry in their bellies growing skin.
The cat sleeps in the backyard,
gray mitten in burnt grass waiting

for something warm to come
within reach. Without warning
your pain starts all its drums beating again.

How does it feel to know your body
is rotten, house with termites, lovely
on the outside but inside

nothing left
but holy and ridiculous hope?

Time Remaining

Time remaining: less than a minute.
The final message
as the computer finishes a download.
Scanning one photo doesn't take long,

but there are many. I name folders:
Kathy. David. Travel. Christmas.
Time remaining:
no scan has been able to tell us. It's a daily

recalibration. You are here today, so it seems
you will be here tomorrow,
even as seconds take flight, like the starlings on a wire
in this vacation snapshot I took thirty years ago.

Inside a Tumor

Pollution, no symmetry,
equations unbalanced, no proofs.
Unhappy mobs, endless waiting
in line, crumbs and carpenter
ants, traffic jams, morning
headaches, curses, no flowers.
Too much aftershave, mud,
spit, black algae, weed slime
that won't wash away. No regard
for the belly, the penis, the scalp.
No clean towels, no good
shoes, rubber on fire,
whistling of dwarves, yellow
breath, badly cut lumber. No A
to any Q, no treasure to hide
in your hand, no keys minor
or silver, no memory of any child.
Nothing that tastes like wine.
No Sundays, Januarys, Junes.

Thanksgiving

Ridiculous,
your fingers,
elevated
to instruments,

thoughtful, delicate,
impossibly clever
as they complete
the dullest tasks.

Not fair—you
pull a cork, blot
a bead of sweat,
and you are in

the spotlight. As if
you are the only one
worth talking to.
We do not wish on you

the failing of your flesh,
but still the fevered
blur of you alive
turns every head.

Our eyes find paths
to meet without you—
as if you are the feast
spread on this table.

As if you are
already memory.

Black Friday

Dream: Parade balloon.
You, serene above cold concrete.
Cheers. Balloon

filled with your breath, tethered
to many hands. Two balloon walkers gripping each tether,
each costumed to look like me—

gray ponytail, purple mittens,
watery eyes peering into wind.
When I wake, you are downstairs.

I bring tea, another blanket,
turn the radio on, off.
You fall asleep, leaving me to walk the house

as if doors cannot be opened.
I stand at each window as the neighborhood comes out
of holiday stupor. Mail truck. Basketball pounding. Brief patter of rain.

Dead leaves pirouette into the street. You shift and snort,
only the top of your red cap showing. Parade balloon.
Air, skin, sky.

Advent

In the long dark that leads
to the end of the year, we rest
with the television on. I drink tea
and brandy and you wrap yourself
in blankets, shiver, sleep. The news
is never good, though sometimes
it tries to be, particularly as we pass
through Christmas. We know
there are colored lights, bonfires
and singing elsewhere in town,
but our world is this room,
peaceful with the noise
of clocks and the few words
between us. Upstairs the bed
is cold. The cat comes in,
snow melting off her back.
She settles on the heat vent,
lets the warm air rise around her,
watches us like we're dangerous.

Circus Train

Five months we've traveled, no landmarks,
gorillas and elephants in every room.
Now and then a tent raised, my greasepaint smile
melting under hot lights. No matter how long we rehearse

we can't get our act right—you fall,
I break a glass. A cat slips into the arena,
crying to be fed as if nothing else is important.
Our audience arrives, anxious

for the show. Neighbors, doctors, cousins,
coworkers, friends. If they cheer us,
maybe we'll get to stay
in this nowhere town a little longer.

Time Remaining

Your body is a science
experiment—all hypotheses,
no promises. Pills and failed pills
rattle in plastic like pieces of bone
in reliquaries. Your tongue has turned

into clay. Sweat forms a Dead Sea
crust on your skin. Hundred-dollar lotions,
compression socks, silk underwear—magic tricks
of medicine. A piece of steel the size of a nickel
set underneath your collarbone is portal

for the drugs with their mighty names
and powers that go awry. Some dust
to make you sleep. Some drink
to make you writhe. Counting backwards

is impossible. Your body
scratches each match-head second
of time remaining, holds on
until it burns.

Waikiki

From the hotel room made of windows,
I watch my husband and son wander out of sight.
I pull the curtains wide, let in everything—

shouts of children swimming in the lagoon,
cigar smoke from the next balcony, fat slap of waves
on tired sand. Somewhere they walk

through a conversation with no room in it for me.
I slide open a door, and the red-capped sparrows
that nest in the balconies step with caution over the threshold.

Six of them, like brothers. Our breakfast crumbs are on the carpet.
I have no superstitions about birds indoors. The boundary
between in and out is gone for me here.

Life into death will be like that for my husband. My son and I
are more like the sparrows—frightening
ourselves with our yearning to see what's inside.

Cooking with Garlic in Barcelona

One good knife in the studio apartment, and I used it
at every meal—to slice oranges and bananas in the almost-afternoon,
when we finally rose for breakfast, for bread and cheese

to stave off hunger until midnight dinnertime. To peel and slice
onions and garlic for the strong stews I kept simmering. Two or three
heads of garlic a day, more than I ever chopped at home. All those cloves

breaking away like sons setting out from families to find a new world.
The smell of garlic cooking in good Spanish olive oil sweeter
than the smell of standing water in the shower drain,

dust burning on the space heater. Perfume
compared to the smell rising from the street, even as the street cleaners
crashed through at 4 a.m. to hose the night's trash away.

I didn't know the Catalan word for garlic when we arrived, but learned it
my first visit to the market. *All.* Winning a smile from the counterman.
Everything I cooked tasted wonderful, restored us back to the city,

the crowds, for another night that wouldn't end until dawn, another morning
weighted by hangover. A year later, you are in our bedroom, dying.
One morning, I take all the vegetables from the bin to make soup—

limp carrots, celery with spots, sprouting onions. I peel garlic,
line cloves up for smashing on the cutting board
where they shine like teeth, like pills, like little lamps.

Dying in Church

In the church of the art museum, you linger
before each painting, breathe into your blood
the vintage ochres and crimsons
of dead genius. Your time has been halved
and halved again. Light falls
on the flowers and fields of centuries
that ended before we were born.

*

We lean hard on our walking sticks
as we climb into the church of the forest.
The shadows of needles pattern our skin.
Leaves bat the brims of our hats.
The view is of where we started,
but it changes when the wind blows
into someplace we have never been.

*

We walk the church of the shopping mall
with other citizens of winter, reflections
that mar window displays, footsteps that clap
on marble cleaned overnight. Later, pretty girls
will trade money for red lips and sexy shoes.
We link arms. I feel the new sharpness
of your elbow, count down the laps.

*

There is no worship anymore in the church of our bed.
We are a chamber in need of restoration.
No Michelangelo holds our miracle, no Gaudi,
even with his most shocking Catalonian dreams.
There are no more prescriptions for us—
no busted hives or pomegranate stairwells
to unwind. We remember the spark of creation,
honey, red juice, but do not talk of it.
Our bed is for silence, sleeping. It creaks
with the weight of midnight, not prayer.

Sad Hotel

Sunny columns fall through skylights.
Bright as pillowcases, clouds pass.
In between alive and dead,

you nod or try to speak.
Alone with you at night,
I talk. It is like dropping

words into a well. I read you
the mail, the hospice notebook
of menus and regulations,

tell you the story
of our marriage with all
the stupid things left out.

Hour of Lead

Quarter till ten, Saturday night,
lines out the doors of good restaurants,
bands tuning up in bars.
Your face like stone on the pillows,

your breath the huffing of an infant asleep.
A nurse does everything for you —
smoothes balm on your lips, feeds you
sips of water from a tiny sponge,

wets and combs the wisps of your hair.
This is a comfort factory,
and product flows hot
like melted caramel. Tonight,

I want you to know I'm here,
sense the healthy thrum of my presence.
All I have, my presence.
That, and I'm the only one

who's noticed you're wearing your glasses.
I lift them from your nose, fold them
on the bedside table as if tomorrow
you'll reach to put them on.

Time Remaining

Days begin with lists
of things it might be nice

to do, and undone
don't harm anyone.

Page to turn. Broom
to move across a sunny,

dusty floor. It is August;
the garden must have

its drink of water.
The cat needs her bowl

filled, her fee for staying on
as my gray shadow.

In this new house
where I live alone, the rooms

are in the same arrangement
as the rooms we shared,

the furniture in place,
shabby. But the cups

gathered in the dark of cabinets
are having a different conversation.

They don't get out as often—their purpose
hasn't changed, but something has happened

that no one has explained
in cup language.

How Do You Lose

someone you know everything about? Utterly.
And not at all. You slow down
on that stretch of highway with the long curve

where he always told you to slow down. Pour the third glass of wine
with his tired joke—the bottle wanted emptying.
There are surprises—

a prayer book in a jacket pocket, a good night's sleep
topped off with a minute of waking
without remembering. Best of all, a dream

of a hard and long embrace, for days the comfort of it
available as a sweater tossed over a chair.
But weeks begin and end,

and there is still a space not quite empty
at the table, a clouded presence always
in another room. As summer withers,

morning, like an old dog, remains expectant
of some touch or kindness coming
that does not come.

4

*You must habit yourself to the dazzle of the light
and of every moment of your life.*

—Walt Whitman

Living in the Marriage Museum

In the dark at the back of a drawer, the envelope
holding the handwritten vows full of magic
we never used. Locked in a box in a safe, the license
to love until death. Past the paper of the first year,
the lobster anniversary, the circular staircase to ten
and twenty and beyond, artifacts accumulated,
silent and solid, in every room. The cherished
and the needed. Kneaded by cat claws and stained

by dogs—rugs, pillows, lamps as individual as aunts,
bronzed and fat, hated and bald. Cups crowded
toward the back of shelves like subway commuters,
rattling hip-to-hip as the vacuum cleaner passes.
Dishes in stacks, tureens and platters
let out only for parties. Jars of preserves—
eternal. In one kitchen drawer, nothing related,

like a class of children from houses all over town—
book of matches the offspring of a barfly and waitress,
AAA batteries from the polite union of a nurse
and engineer. Avalanche of stale ice in the freezer.
In a basket, clean coffee spoons, silver rustle
each morning, mirrors cupped to catch the light.
From the kitchen, the galleries spiral—garage, dining room,
living room, each with its ephemera. Spindle-legged desk

with seashells and scissors, notepads, scribbled and blank.
Photos in frames, rack of wine bottles, candles with cindered wicks,
toolbox, rocking chair. In the hall closet, in the pocket
of his winter coat, a wool hat that smells like unwashed hair.
A pinecone on the mantel, a Menorah. The bathroom mirror—
pinwheels of satisfaction and dissatisfaction and nothing and desire.
Behind glass, precious things from distant places.

Music in stacks. Acoustic guitar. Fourteen harmonicas
in various keys. Keys. Coins. Belt buckles. Provocative
underwear I hated. Twenty pairs of his shoes. The soft wool sleeve

of a sweater. The tight knit cuffs of a gray shirt
with a pattern of fish. Plastic, wood, glass, wool, string, paper,
tin, splinters, thread, dust, ash. Eight pounds of ash
in a plastic case. Encased. The basement is filled

with bucket smells and swift shadows. The corridors are endless
at night, alarms set, lights on and off. I have taken the ring
off my finger, to concede the miracle of the ending
of the vows. I have taken the roof off the bedroom.
The bed is a lake. It will swell in spring when it rains,
in summer shrink in the heat. Come winter,
I'll sleep with a blanket of ice.

Night Knitting

Always good to have a row cast on—the night will come
when I'll need the reassurance of brown or purple wool,
needles' industry between sleeplessness and the immensity

of the world asleep. Even if snow is knitting its own caps and capes,
even if wind is undoing every knot,
I will have a pool of lamplight,

the back of a soft chair like an arm around my shoulders.
As I sit wishing for someone to talk to,
I will have the small stitches to count,

the clack-of-bone conversation, the thing—
what is it?—
falling from my hands.

Out in the Cold

1. New Year's Eve

Between the end of Christmas and the restarting of the engine of another year
is today. *Happy New Year!* friends shout at my party. Food and drink and dark.
Magic and secret as we stand out in the yard, stars of snow falling into our hair.
Fireworks thud in the distance, sparks hang in clouds like Christmas lights.
I pour champagne. Someone starts a song but falters a short way in—
too many verses no one can remember. The sky looks like the ice of a pond.
We press our faces close, try to make out the other side.

2. New Year's Day

Shards of cold and crystal catch in my throat.
My hair crackles. The fountain outside church
is draped in a heavy cover, bark mulch raked around skeletons
of roses, veins of fallen oak leaves traced white by frost.
I stand at the stone set here last summer.
Two words that make up my husband's name.
Two numbers that make up the span of his life.
This is the second turning of a year without him.
Cold rises into my clothes. This moment of sunlight
holds no more grace than any other.

3. Twelfth Night

Snow on grass. Sundown a lavender
and ruby cloud combed across the west.
Mad scented crush of December gone.
I have not so much arrived
as been delivered to this day.
Vapors from neighbors' chimneys
twist into the wind and fade.

4. Epiphany

Snow makes everything look small—the lake with frozen banks
encroaching, the cabin low among the trees. The lock resists my key.
Floors echo my steps. So many things to be packed away.
Coolers and camp chairs, rods and reels. Our big box of fishing tackle,
hooks and lures neatly sorted, gutting knife gleaming sharp.
The *For Sale* sign goes up tomorrow. I open drawers,
shake moths from blankets, chase silverfish out of frying pans.
The old guitar has snapped a string. The radio is cracked.
When I unlatch the wood stove, a smell thick as smoke fills the room—
a dead squirrel in the wreckage of our last fire. I toss it out,
leave the back door open. The kitchen bristles with the chill.
On a bare mattress I nap and dream a sunny morning, my husband sleeping
as I get up to make coffee. When I return, the bedroom door is locked.
I knock, he doesn't answer. Something scratches
on the other side. The knob rattles. That is all.

Shelf Life

My father calls me because I have forgotten to call him.
I often forget. He will be eighty-seven soon, widowed twelve years.
He has made of it a blossoming, somehow, learned to turn

on the vacuum, change fitted sheets. He makes very good
blueberry pancakes. In his pantry, though, are cans of soup,
bottles of Tangy Italian salad dressing that have been there years past

the dates stamped on their labels. He feels that way, too, some days,
he tells me. Gone are the mornings getting out of bed without aches
in his shoulders and back. The days he could tackle swift-falling snow

with an easy shovel. He plants two tomato seedlings each spring,
in plastic pots set in a child's wagon he bought at a garage sale.
As they grow, he waters, sprays, fertilizes, moves the wagon

with the sun, front yard to back. Good exercise, he says.
In his care, the green stems branch and flower, as patient as he is,
for the August day when the fruit will be ready for his knife.

His Truck

I keep the payments up.
On the dashboard keep the Cardinals cap
as if he's just forgotten it
and will be coming back

the minute the sun lowers
into his eyes. I keep his Navy duffel
on the seat beside me packed
with not much. Mornings

in new places—all those fresh blues
the sky can be, the rain
a different scent depending
on the time of day. I traced

the Maine coast in a week, salty plumes
of fog slanting off pine bluffs, rimed
yellow flowers. I lingered
in a Carolina town hemmed in

by tobacco fields—streets paved
with oyster shells, alleys fragrant
with cooking through open screens—
dough and meat taking their turns

in cast iron pans, burners ringing.
Everywhere, I hear things
I never have—arguments at gas pumps,
hill birds calling to shore birds,

traffic thrumming on highways miles away.
I've learned to sleep in unfamiliar beds,
drive into the sun without a map,
hold the road in storms—

torrents of rain trying to break
the windshield. I can change
a flat with a pen light in my teeth,
ask for anything I want.

An Argument for Going On

The autumn we hiked in Zion, my husband brought his harmonica,
      played as he stepped stone to stone, *O-Bla-Di,* through a creek,
            O-Bla-Da. Each note like a leaf, yellow, red, lifted

along blazing rock. Above us men climbed the cliff's featureless face,
      holding the blankness so close it embraced them.
            Every embrace is a blankness. In the canyon

of anyone's arms, there is nothing to see, only a rising to feel—
      weightlessness, leaves into wind—and nothing to hear,
            except, from below, the slippery notes of an old song.

Travel

In the end, even the good trips turn out to be about everything
you didn't do, every place you didn't go. Photographs sorted
and stowed, empty pages where the view around the curve,

the smile across the room were meant to be.
You come home with regrets like the curled stubs of tickets
in your pockets, no recollection of where you left the afternoon

drinking black beer with the pair of retired math teachers
and the man who sang like Bob Dylan. You walked away
and forgot it like an umbrella when the rain stopped,

but you remember there is no place more wet
than the concrete stair to a waterfront bar in the rain.
Time is constantly tipping its hat to you. Moon that was full

leaves a kiss on your pillow. You pack up the woolly sweater,
jaunty cap, the sunglasses that make you look sexy.
You say good-bye to the jade hills, the whap of waves

on the shore. Your license as an imposter is expired.
In the airport, you promise yourself you'll never forget
how to say *thank you* in Greek or the name of that orange flower.

Sight

His last week alive, my father saw everything clearly.
Every day a girl came, made breakfast, counted out pills
for his heart. Eyes open or closed, he saw himself

in perfect focus in every mirror. Without my mother,
darkness had become as illuminating as light. The walls
of the wide stair to the bedroom drew close to his shoulders.

He saw webbed cracks and fingerprints, shadows of swatted flies.
In the bathroom, his facecloth rose like a bird
to hover at his cheek. Sitting in his television chair,

chewing the butt of an unlit cigar, his reflection in the black screen
showed him a man who might as well be young—a man alone
in a sagging chair who didn't know what to do with his hands.

A stream of water at the kitchen sink loosed words from old songs
that broke on the porcelain. My mother's face leaked
with the blue flame from the burner on the stove. At the table,

he read not the newspaper or the mail, but the messages she'd left
on the tablecloth—decades of soup spills and batter smears,
plate thumps and whiskey pours. Where she once sat across from him, he saw

the flakes of her skin, rime of her tears, the shards, feathers, smooth pebbles
of their conversations. He wanted nothing more than to lean across
and sweep everything to him like the crumbs of a Christmas feast.

After All

In your later seasons, no one loves you,
unless you've had the sense
to stick with the same complaining woman

or gassy old man, watching the hairs
fall out of his head or grow on her chin.
Do you even love you anymore, or are you too much trouble

after all—grunting out of bed, hunting for a pair of socks to put on?
There is one sock under the dresser, but the other is lost.
For breakfast you make toast, scrape the black away,

then use the knife to spread butter and jam.
Black crumbs scatter everywhere, like ants that wait for you
to turn your back so they can smother everything in your house.

You remember spring. And summer. (Summer!)
You have no memories of hunger, rain, night predators
howling from hill to hill. You have a stick that lets you lean on it,

down the path and back every day. You have a pot of geraniums
in the kitchen window. Every morning you find a fizzled bloom or two
dropped on the sill, a gift, though not exactly.

Lazarus

You rise from the dead to empty the dishwasher, wearing the tweed cap
you gave my brother's second son, the only one of his three boys who went

to college. He got an English degree from some school in Kansas and
now washes cars for Avis at the Joplin airport and curses vividly about slobs

who smoke and eat nachos in rental vehicles. You rise like the mermaid
my friend has dropped into the middle of his book of short stories.

I have told him twice that she is mealy-mouthed and mechanical, too bitter
and cold-blooded for anyone to love, even the widowed fisherman

who has stopped mending his nets, who bangs out the bowl of his pipe
in the sink and stares at the cuts on his fingers. The next story

in my friend's manuscript is much better. It contains a reference to the movie
that is the soft-porn version of *Alice in Wonderland.* Instead of shouting,

Off with his head, the Red Queen shouts, *Give me some head.*
I remember this movie. You and I went to see it before we got married.

We confessed we liked the scene with Tweedledum and Tweedledee
better than the one with Alice and the Red Queen. You rise

like the flying fish we happened on as we hiked past a nameless lake
in Oregon. We had heard of flying fish, and here they were,

leaving the water to perform their modest loops, in no way the flyers
that birds are or even Chinese acrobats. I would have named them

splashing fish, I said, as their flat eyes trapped sunlight and they fell
helplessly back into the dark. It was July. Snow was melting on the trail.

You rise like that, into dreams and memories, into air
burdened with silence—miraculous, unbelievable, brief.

I Wake in My Father's Bed

Solids from shadows emerge—
mirror, empty shelf, closet door.
Sky not yet morning blue, a distant

shout down in the street. Tired
as if I haven't slept, tangled
in the weeds of his quilt, a slow awakening

on the strewn beach of another day.
Furnace thump. Airplane overhead.
Dreams fading to lists, instructions,

plans. Sour thirst in my mouth,
throb at the bottom of my spine,
paycheck for yesterday's work—

so many boxes to pack, so many books
for a man who didn't read. Hooks hidden
in buckets of tackle—knotted line,

rusted reels, fingers pricked. So much glass,
sawdust, so many oily parts of tools
even my brother couldn't name.

Decades since he closed the shop,
moved far away from any shore.
Not even Goodwill wanted his shirts,

flannel worn to the fineness of ash,
cracked buttons, the reek of his daily cigar.
A body crumbles; a soul flees. Someone must

finish the work that the landlord, the government,
the electric company require. Vacated rooms
left to their dusty breathing, the creeping of sun

down walls and into corners. This morning
has been waiting a long time. The light
is weak, finding its way to me.

To Anne Sexton

When I was sixteen, I wanted to be you,
and I wanted you to be my mother. I thought
girls needed gin, not cocoa, to grow up with courage.
I envied your long legs, your cigarettes, your black,
unyielding hair. My heart clutched at your slyness
with acrostics, the unapologetic appetites
brought down on you by madness, brilliance, luck—
all interchangeable once you'd put on makeup
and had a weeping cold glass in your hand.
You slapped the men who needed slapping
and lay down with the men you needed
on lumpy mattresses or towels damp with ocean water.
When Sylvia died, babies asleep, furniture
crammed against the door, and up and down the stairs
snow melted in the prints of policemen's boots,
you said *That death was mine* and I understood
it was not a sin for women to aspire
to each other's bitterness, borrow rage
as if it were a tube of lipstick or a comb.

Before

I was an egg in two parts in my grandmother's hand. I was an apple
in my grandfather's hand. In the flood of a dream, I was the quavering
face of a stone. In a glass bowl, swaddled in a white towel, I was three
eggs that whispered to each other the old stories—wishes, black brooms,
earth that crumbled like cake in the mouths of lost children. I was the long
peel of an apple ratcheted over a blade. I was my grandmother's apron
with its stain in the shape of an egg, my grandfather's clean handkerchief
stamped into a perfect square under the weight of an iron. I was the black net
purse in my grandmother's hand inside the silk of her glove, the space
inside of her hand as she took my grandfather's hand the first time
he asked her to dance. Waiting for spring, I slept furled in the magnolia
blossom. All night I tapped at the kitchen window, waiting
for my pink hood to drop. I was the eye in the bowl of the rain barrel,
blinking with each drop of rain, witness to everything.

The Thin Place

Before sleep, I see them—my grandparents,
their sisters and brothers—maids, taxi drivers,
elevator operators, factory girls who pinched my cheeks
and teased me about growing tall, sent me birthday cards
with nickels taped inside. The women cooked with grease,
onions, hot paprika, sprinkled cabbage with caraway seeds.
The men lifted me into their laps, belched in my face,
offered me sips of beer. Tonight the table is set

with the chrysanthemum plates. Coffee is boiling,
the silver tongs rest in the sugar bowl. My mother
and father are with them tonight. My husband
walks up the driveway, leaf shadows rippling
over his clothes. He has a bottle of wine in one hand,
in the other a bakery box tied with red string.

❧ ∽

Acknowledgments

I am grateful to the journals in which earlier versions of these poems appeared:

Apple Valley Review: "Come Inside"

Bellevue Literary Review: "Stage Four, Summer," "Advent"

Blood Orange Review: "Before"

Breakwater Review: "Waking in My Father's Bed"

Comstock Review: "The Women in the Kitchen," "Drop a Knife, Somebody's Coming," "Maybe This World," "Travel"

Escape into Life: "Adam and Eve," "How It Rained in Barcelona," "Waikiki," "Night Knitting," "Lady of the House," "Mother Song"

Inkwell: "Phone Call from a Movie Set Somewhere in Kansas"

Moon City Review: "Polly's Mother Sang Opera"

poemeleon: "Kiss"

qarrtsiluni: "In the Middle of the Night"

REAL: "Boys Who Cut the Legs Off Box Turtles," "What Is Love?"

Schuykill Valley Journal: "I Speak at My Mother's Funeral"

Smoky Blue Literary and Arts Magazine: "How Do You Lose," "First Communion Day," "Dreams of Dead Women"

South 85: "Homecoming"

Spoon River Poetry Review: "Soup"

Stone Canoe: "To Anne Sexton"

About FutureCycle Press

FutureCycle Press is dedicated to publishing lasting English-language poetry books, chapbooks, and anthologies in both print-on-demand and Kindle ebook formats. Founded in 2007 by long-time independent editor/publishers and partners Diane Kistner and Robert S. King, the press incorporated as a nonprofit in 2012. A number of our editors are distinguished poets and writers in their own right, and we have been actively involved in the small press movement going back to the early seventies.

The FutureCycle Poetry Book Prize and honorarium is awarded annually for the best full-length volume of poetry we publish in a calendar year. Introduced in 2013, our Good Works projects are anthologies devoted to issues of universal significance, with all proceeds donated to a related worthy cause. Our Selected Poems series highlights contemporary poets with a substantial body of work to their credit; with this series we strive to resurrect work that has had limited distribution and is now out of print.

We are dedicated to giving all of the authors we publish the care their work deserves, making our catalog of titles the most diverse and distinguished it can be, and paying forward any earnings to fund more great books.

We've learned a few things about independent publishing over the years. We've also evolved a unique, resilient publishing model that allows us to focus mainly on vetting and preserving for posterity poetry collections of exceptional quality without becoming overwhelmed with bookkeeping and mailing, fundraising activities, or taxing editorial and production "bubbles." To find out about what we are doing, come see us at www.futurecycle.org.

The FutureCycle Poetry Book Prize

All full-length volumes of poetry published by FutureCycle Press in a given calendar year are considered for the annual FutureCycle Poetry Book Prize. This allows us to consider each submission on its own merits, outside of the context of a contest. Too, the judges see the finished book, which will have benefitted from the beautiful book design and strong editorial gloss we are famous for.

The book ranked the best in judging is announced as the prize-winner in the subsequent year. There is no fixed monetary award; instead, the winning poet receives an honorarium of 20% of the total net royalties from all poetry books and chapbooks the press sold online in the year the winning book was published. The winner is also accorded the honor of being on the panel of judges for the next year's competition; all judges receive copies of all contending books to keep for their personal library.